D1709792

EXPLORING HI-TECH JOBS

# Hi-Tech Jobs in
# MEDICAL
# TECHNOLOGY

Leanne Currie-McGhee

ReferencePoint
Press

San Diego, CA

LIBRARY OF CONGRESS CATALOGING-IN-PUBLICATION DATA

Names: Currie-McGhee, L. K. (Leanne K.), author.
Title: Hi-tech jobs in medical technology / by Leanne Currie-McGhee.
Description: San Diego, CA : ReferencePoint Press, Inc., 2024. | Series:
    Exploring hi-tech jobs | Includes bibliographical references and index.
Identifiers: LCCN 2023034250 (print) | LCCN 2023034251 (ebook) | ISBN
    9781678207045 (library binding) | ISBN 9781678207052 (ebook)
Subjects: LCSH: Biomedical technicians--Vocational guidance--Juvenile
    literature. | Biomedical engineers--Vocational guidance--Juvenile
    literature. | Medical technology--Juvenile literature.
Classification: LCC R856.25 .C87 2024 (print) | LCC R856.25 (ebook) | DDC
    610.285--dc23/eng/20230901
LC record available at https://lccn.loc.gov/2023034250
LC ebook record available at https://lccn.loc.gov/2023034251

# Contents

# Introduction: Technology in Medicine Equals Jobs

Medical technology is advancing by leaps and bounds. To keep up with all of these changes, or in some cases to create the technology that is changing the practice of medicine, many workers will be needed in the coming years. Engineers will be needed in the ongoing efforts to develop surgical robots, diagnostic equipment, cutting edge prosthetics, drug delivery systems, and more. Technologists and technicians, who are already doing various types of imaging and testing, will continue to fill essential jobs. Scientists and doctors who assess samples, scans, and tests aimed at diagnosing and treating a wide array of ailments will also continue to be in demand.

## New Ideas Lead to Job Growth

Possibly the biggest area of job growth in connection with technology and medicine is in artificial intelligence (AI). AI-enabled technology, sometimes referred to as machine learning, is already being tested in the medical field—in research, drug development and testing, disease identification, and personalized patient care. Although predictions of AI in medicine often raise concerns about job losses, some experts say the likelihood of job growth in this field is actually very high. Information technology professor Ashok K. Harnal writes in the *Economic Times* of India:

The rapid growth of technology and its incorporation into the healthcare system was initially seen as a threat to human jobs, but in reality it has opened up endless job opportunities. Undoubtedly, technology is automating repetitive jobs, but this does not imply that human intervention is no longer necessary. Someone who possesses an in-depth knowledge of technology and understands its application is needed to oversee machine [learning] operations.[1]

AI represents a new and growing career field in medicine, but that does not mean other technology-related careers are slowing. Engineers are designing new and more sophisticated surgical robots, for instance. At Johns Hopkins University, engineers are developing a robot that could one day be used to stitch together blood vessels, organs, and other soft tissue without a surgeon's direct involvement. The robot, which is still experimental, has one arm equipped with a camera and the other with hi-tech suturing instruments. Once a surgeon makes an incision, the robot uses its machine learning algorithms and computer vision to create a surgical plan as it "sees" the patient's organs and tissue. It carries out that plan by itself, using input from the camera. The goal is to reduce human error in surgical procedures, particularly those that require precision and repetitive motion.

Biomedical engineering is another profession that will continue to be in demand in the health care industry. "Global health engineering may not be sexy, but it saves lives," says Madhukar Pai, a writer who focuses on global health. This became evident during the COVID-19 pandemic. According to Pai, "During this crisis, engineers have made huge contributions by delivering oxygen, oxygen concentrators, pulse oximeters, ventilators, rapid tests, high-filtration masks, air purifiers, vaccine cold chains, logistics, supply chain management, mobile apps, [and] data dashboards, among other things."[2]

## Technology-Focused Jobs
## Bring New Job Opportunities

On a daily basis, health care professionals at all levels use technology for diagnosis, treatment, and many other aspects of patient care. This translates to steady growth in technology-focused jobs throughout the health care industry. These jobs include people who are trained to do various types of sophisticated imaging. They will also need people trained to work in relatively new fields such as theranostics. Theranostics combines imaging with molecular radiotherapy. Its goal is to identify cancerous tumors and then target just those tumors for treatment without harming nearby tissue, as often occurs in more traditional cancer treatment. Dmitry Beyder, a certified nuclear medicine technologist, believes advances like this will bring about exciting career opportunities in the medical field. "I expect to see some great techniques and opportunities arise over the next 10 to 20 years," says Beyder. "We need excited and hard-working people to join the workforce, eager to learn and do, and this will be an amazing career for them."[3]

Whether you are interested in developing technology or working with it, there are many careers in the medical field to consider. In these fields, you could be developing a vaccine to fight a virus, testing a medical device that tracks pulse rate and blood pressure, or performing a test that records brain activity. From working directly with patients to researching in a laboratory, hi-tech careers in the medical field provide exciting challenges and options for aspiring youth.

# Biomedical Engineer

## What Does a Biomedical Engineer Do?

Biomedical engineers combine expertise in biology, medicine, and engineering to develop medical devices, equipment, and other technologies used for diagnosis and treatment of a wide variety of illnesses and conditions. Some biomedical engineers design prosthetics for people who have lost limbs. Others develop artificial organs to replace diseased or damaged ones. Some biomedical engineers are involved in the development of software that runs diagnostic tools such as 3-D X-ray machines. Still others design or improve drug delivery systems that control where drugs are released in the body and the amount and speed of release. The paths within the field of biomedical engineering are varied, providing many possible career options.

Natalia Trayanova is a professor of biomedical engineering at Johns Hopkins University, where her lab focuses on developing virtual hearts. Virtual hearts are computer models that accurately depict a person's entire heart. The models can be used to predict how certain situations, such as a clot in an artery, will affect

## A Few Facts

**Number of Jobs**
About 17,900 in 2021

**Pay**
Median annual salary of
$108,060 in 2022

**Educational Requirements**
Bachelor's degree in biomedical engineering or biomedical science; Professional Engineer certification preferred

**Personal Qualities**
Innovative, logical, detail oriented

**Work Settings**
Laboratories with companies or academic and research institutions

**Future Job Outlook**
Growth rate of 10 percent through 2031

the heart. "In my lab, we use the power of predictive simulations to generate personalized virtual hearts for diagnostic purposes and also for devising the best treatment for a given patient,"[4] Trayanova explains. She and her colleagues have developed computer simulations of heart disease, for instance. Doctors can use simulations to develop appropriate treatment plans for patients. Biomedical engineers like Trayanova are at the forefront of creating a future where the latest technology—in this case, computer simulations—will guide patient care.

## A Typical Workday

Saloni Verma is a biomedical engineer at Rheonix, a molecular diagnostic company in upstate New York. At Rheonix she was initially involved in the development of automated molecular assays. Automated molecular assays are a type of diagnostic testing that uses equipment programmed to test human tissue samples (such as blood or saliva) for medical conditions such as the human immunodeficiency virus, hepatitis, or COVID-19. In recent years Verma has been involved with the design and development of the Rheonix assay used for diagnostic testing of COVID-19.

Development of any molecular assay is a lengthy process, since it involves finding a way to isolate specific molecules in the

## Gain Experience

"Co-ops and internships in industry and research experiences in labs at the undergraduate level make a huge difference in both understanding the work and in finding jobs and deciding on whether to pursue graduate work."

—Erin Lavik, biomedical engineer

Quoted in Emily Bratcher, "Biomedical Engineer Overview," *U.S. News & World Report*, 2023. https://money.usnews.com.

Biomedical engineers develop medical devices (such as prostheses, as shown here), as well as technologies used for diagnosis and treatment of a wide variety of illnesses and conditions.

specimens to determine the presence of a disease. Design and testing typically take more than a year's worth of work. During the design process, biomedical engineers spend many days in the laboratory, using chemical reactions and other means to isolate the molecule. Then they set up and program the equipment to perform specific tasks to test for the molecule on many samples at once. During the testing phase, biomedical engineers run the testing system on samples, study the results, and determine whether the system is accurate by comparing the results to those of other types of testing methods.

The work of biomedical engineers does not stop after a testing system is approved for use. They often assist with setup and operation as well as making continued improvements based on feedback from their customers. On a typical day, Verma might go to a lab that uses one of her company's molecular testing systems. She might help a new client with setup of the system, or she might watch how the testing systems are being used at the lab and offer suggestions for improving results. "In the last two years I've shifted to . . . managing the products that are already out there, identifying the scope of where we can improve them, and then . . . laying out a plan of action,"[5] says Verma.

Some biomedical engineers work directly with patients, doctors, and nurses. Their job is to make sure medical devices are being properly used and working as intended. A biomedical engineer named Rah works for a company that develops implantable cardiac devices such as pacemakers and defibrillators. Rah's workdays include visits to hospital operating rooms and patients' rooms. During an operation involving one of her company's devices, she offers advice to medical staff and answers any questions they have about the device. With patients, she makes sure the device is working properly and provides training on how to monitor, care for, and use the device. Her day may include looking in on up to ten surgeries as well as several patient visits.

Not all biomedical engineers work directly with clients or patients. Some, like Alexa Perozo, actually test new devices to find out what works and what needs improvement. Perozo's company makes health care simulators, models of people designed to give an accurate representation of human anatomy. The simulators display physiological signs, such as a heart rate, through computer systems. This allows places like medical and nursing schools to use them for instruction. "When a new product is ready to be released," she says, "I test it out, and I go back to the design team and let them know what is working and what can be done better."[6]

## Education and Training

Not surprisingly, academic requirements for this type of work are heavy on math and science. High school students who are interested in this field can get a head start by taking Advanced Placement math and science courses, particularly in biology and chemistry. Obtaining a four-year degree with a major in biomedical engineering or biomedical science is essential.

The field is competitive, so obtaining a master's degree and PhD will give a person a greater chance of breaking into the industry. Obtaining a professional certification is also helpful in getting hired as a biomedical engineer. To obtain this, you must first pass the Fundamentals of Engineering exam offered by the National Council of Examiners for Engineering and Surveying, which tests your knowledge of the math and science needed to complete most engineering work. Passing the second exam, taken after working as an engineer for four years, will allow you to obtain a license in the Principles and Practice of Engineering.

## Skills and Personality

An aptitude for math, science, and problem solving are all essential for anyone who works in biomedical engineering. Math and scientific principles are the foundation of design and development of all medical technology. Problem-solving skills often come into play during development and testing. For example, when developing a medical device such as a pacemaker, if there is a problem with it staying charged, one has to be able to determine what is not working and how to fix it. Tied to this, one should be an out-of-the-box thinker, able to come up with solutions when different types of problems arise. The ability to keep track of details without losing sight of the big picture is also important. A biomedical engineer who is developing a prosthetic hand, for example, needs to make sure each finger works properly and that the fingers and thumb work together for correct hand function.

## Working Conditions

Biomedical engineers work in a variety of settings. They work in hospitals and government offices, universities and research labs, and manufacturing facilities. No matter which setting they work in, most biomedical engineers spend large chunks of time at their computer as they develop, test, and improve medical devices or equipment and document their work. Those who work in hospitals spend time with patients and medical professionals, often donning scrubs and a mask as they observe surgeries involving the devices or equipment their company has developed. Those in laboratories may work in clean rooms to prevent contamination of devices or experiments. A clean room uses filtration devices to remove airborne particles, and all staff wear gowns, hairnets, and overshoes to reduce the chance of contamination.

Biomedical engineering is a cooperative venture. Engineers work closely with life scientists, chemists, laboratory technicians, and medical professionals. They collaborate with them on different areas during the design and development process of devices, systems, or other types of medical products.

Hours vary depending on where a biomedical engineer works. Those in companies or institutes typically work normal weekday hours. Those in hospitals or other medical facilities may be on call and working days and nights or longer shifts.

## Employers and Earnings

According to the Bureau of Labor Statistics (BLS), 28 percent of biomedical engineers work in research and development in physical, engineering, and life sciences, while 14 percent work in medical equipment and supplies manufacturing. "You can work in industry, academia, and government. The doors are wide open,"[7] says biomedical engineer Irene Bacalocostantis. In her job with the US Food and Drug Administration, Bacalocostantis reviews the safety and efficacy of medical devices used in gastroenterology, an area of medicine focused on the digestive system and related disorders.

Biomedical engineers are highly paid. In 2022, the BLS reports, the median annual salary was $108,060. Experience, education, and location can influence salaries. Those with more experience and advanced degrees tend to earn more money. The same goes for biomedical engineers who work in large cities, such as Phoenix and San Francisco, with active biomedical research communities.

## Future Outlook

As demand for hi-tech medical equipment, devices, and therapies increases, biomedical engineers will likely increase in demand. The BLS projects that biomedical engineering careers will grow by 10 percent through 2031, which is a higher-than-average growth rate for careers. This provides many opportunities for future biomedical engineers. As a result, for any teen who is passionate about science and interested in making a difference in people's lives and health, biomedical engineering is a field to consider.

## Find Out More

**American Institute for Medical and
Biological Engineering (AIMBE)**

https://aimbe.org

The AIMBE is a nonprofit organization that represents people who work in the medical and biomedical engineering fields. Its website provides information about the latest in biomedical engineering. The site also features a "For Students" section that includes biomedical engineering history and videos of biomedical engineers discussing what they do.

**Biomedical Engineering Society**

www.bmes.org

This is a nonprofit professional association whose mission is to promote biomedical engineering knowledge and its use in health care. Its website includes links to various journals about biomedical engineering, membership news, and educational events. There is also a student section that gives information on colleges and high schools with active groups in the society and how to join or form a chapter.

**Engineering in Medicine and Biology Society**

www.embs.org

This is the world's largest organization of biomedical engineers, with over ten thousand members in ninety-seven countries. Its website provides links to publications about biomedical engineering news. It also provides a student section with lists of student conferences and mentorship opportunities.

# EEG Technologist

## What Does an EEG Technologist Do?

When a person experiences seizures, sudden memory loss, severe sleep problems, or head trauma, an electroencephalogram (EEG) test is often ordered to help with diagnosis of the problem. An EEG records and measures the brain's electrical activity, including brain wave patterns and any unusual changes. The person who performs this test is an EEG technologist. The technologist works with patients to prepare them for the test, ensure they are as calm as possible, and explain the process. The technologist conducts the tests and ensures that he or she obtains detailed results in order for doctors to be able to make critical diagnoses.

An EEG technologist, which also can be called a neurodiagnostic technologist, uses the EEG equipment to measure brain abnormalities in patients and monitor nervous system activity to detect brain disorders or anomalies. A technologist's duties include first reviewing the patient's medical history, then explaining the procedure to him or her and answering questions. Next the technologist prepares the patient for the test by attaching electrodes to the

## A Few Facts

**Number of Jobs**
About 329,200 in 2021*

**Pay**
Estimated annual salary of $68,381 in 2023

**Educational Requirements**
Associate's degree; certification by an accredited program recommended

**Personal Qualities**
Personable, precise, organized

**Work Settings**
Hospitals, medical clinics

**Future Job Outlook**
Projected 25,600 openings annually*

* This number is for clinical lab technologists and technicians, which includes EEG technologists.

patient's head in specific areas, based on the size of the head. The technologist ensures the wires from the electrodes are connected correctly to the EEG machine. Then he or she operates the machinery during the test and makes adjustments as needed to get the necessary readings. This may include setting up a long-term test, in which the person remains connected to the EEG machine for a longer time, such as recording when a patient periodically experiences seizures or conducting an overnight sleep test. It is up to the EEG technologist to obtain the crucial information that doctors need to help their patients.

## A Typical Workday

Cathy Konold is an EEG technologist at University of Utah Hospital. Her day starts with finding out who her attending neurologist is. EEG technologists often work closely with neurologists, doctors who specialize in working with the brain and nervous system. The neurologist is who she will send the EEGs to once they are completed. Once she knows who the neurologist is, she prepares for her first patient. Konold explains:

> The test takes about 90 minutes for me to complete. If I have some time before the patient arrives, I review their records to determine the reason the test was ordered, as well as whether the patient might have speech or mobility difficulties. If the patient has been admitted to the hospital, I'll look at other upcoming procedures such as MRI and CT scans. This allows me to coordinate with the patient's nurse if needed, so I can do my test at the best time in relation to other imaging appointments.[8]

Konold likes to complete one to two tests before lunch. In her months as a technologist, she has learned some techniques to make the job easier on the patient. One of these techniques involves placing a paper towel roll under the neck, just below the patient's head, while she determines where to place the electrodes.

"This towel roll is the EEG tech's secret to reaching O1 and O2, which are electrode locations on the back of the head,"[9] says Konold. After lunch, Konold usually performs another test or two on patients. She says her days fly by as she tests patients, prepares for them, or takes time to study new procedures in her field.

Jared Beckwith is also an EEG technologist. He works at a hospital in Tampa, Florida. He usually works a regular schedule of three days a week and is on call one night a week. His regular workdays are twelve-hour shifts. The one night a week he is on call, he must come in if a doctor determines that an EEG is immediately necessary, such as when a person is experiencing seizures. Conducting an EEG usually takes about sixty minutes after setup. However, he sometimes does a continuous monitoring EEG, in which the patient stays hooked up to the EEG to monitor brain activity for an extended period of time. With this type of test, he considers that the patient may need to undergo other tests, such as MRI scans. To make sure all scans can proceed smoothly, he uses special EEG wires and electrodes that do not have to be removed during imaging scans. For both Konold and Beckwith, a successful shift is one in which they obtain the needed tests so that doctors can determine a diagnosis and a plan for the patients.

An EEG technologist attaches electrodes to a patient's head in preparation for an EEG test. These tests measure brain abnormalities and monitor nervous system activity.

## Education and Training

Most EEG technologists obtain training through a one-year program offered at community colleges or hospitals. Those pursuing these programs should ensure they are accredited by the Commission on Accreditation of Allied Health Education Programs. The programs typically include classroom instruction on subjects such as anatomy and electricity. They also include on-the-job training, which typically begins with mannequins and eventually progresses to real patients. Coursework includes proper techniques for taking head measurements, marking the location for electrode placement, and placing electrodes accurately. They also learn how to operate the EEG equipment and to analyze what the wave output shows. After the program, many seek certification as an EEG technologist through the American Board of Registration of Electroencephalographic and Evoked Potential Technicians. To become certified, candidates provide training verification and a cardiopulmonary resuscitation certification, then sit for an exam. The exam is a multiple-choice, four-hour test that covers the material learned in the programs, such as neurological disorders, electrode properties, and waveform analysis.

High school students interested in this career should take classes in biology, chemistry, math, and English. This will help them prepare for the classes in the program. Since these technologists deal with patients, other classes such as psychology and communications can help them develop interpersonal skills.

## Skills and Personality

Worry and even fear are not uncommon emotions in patients who need to undergo EEGs. For this reason, interaction with patients is an important part of the technologist's job. Putting people at ease about the procedure they are about to have is a valuable skill and can be very satisfying. "The best part of my day is trying to make a procedure that can be really scary and stressful, especially for children, be not that way and make it a comfortable experience,"[10] says senior EEG technologist Sharon Carline. Most patients appreciate when the technologist clearly explains what the EEG is, what it does, and how it will work. Clear communication between the technologist and the patient is another way to put patients at ease.

EEG technologists must be precise and detail oriented. Electrodes have to be placed in specific locations on a patient's head, and wires have to be correctly connected to obtain accurate recordings of brain waves and patterns. Technologists need to be comfortable operating and calibrating hi-tech equipment and troubleshooting any issues.

## Working Conditions

As with many health care professionals, EEG technologists often work weekdays in twelve-hour shifts. Some work on call, which can include nights and weekends. Some EEG technologists work as traveling technologists. This means they take contracts to work in a different location, such as at a hospital in another city or state, for a specified amount of time. It could be weeks or even months. They receive a higher salary because they have to travel and find lodging; however, this could mean they forgo certain benefits such as health insurance and paid vacations.

EEG technologists work in busy environments. Much of their time is spent working directly with patients—explaining the procedure and then doing the EEGs. Technologists also spend time cleaning and maintaining the equipment before and after each use. Additionally, they provide the EEG readout and documentation, such as any physiological changes that occurred during the test. As an example, a doctor will want to know whether there were any seizures during the test and when they occurred.

## Employers and Earnings

EEG technologists typically work in hospitals, outpatient treatment centers, sleep clinics, or the offices of neurologists. According to Glassdoor, in June 2023 estimated yearly pay for an EEG technologist was $68,381. EEG technologists with years of experience typically are paid at a higher rate than people with less experience.

## Future Outlook

As with other jobs in the health care industry, there are many opportunities for trained EEG technologists. The Bureau of Labor Statistics projects a growth rate of 7 percent for health technologists, which includes those who specialize in doing EEGs, through 2031. EEG technologists looking for advancement can work toward lead EEG technologist or supervisory positions. For a young person who is interested in spending time with people combined with working on modern technology, this career can be satisfying.

## Find Out More

**American Board of Registration of Electroencephalographic and Evoked Potential Technicians (ABRET)**

https://abret.org

ABRET is a credentialing board for EEG technologists and others in the neurodiagnostic field. It holds certification exams for those in the field who meet all other requirements. On this site, when visiting the "Programs and Education" section, students can learn which schools and health institutions offer accredited programs and learn the paths to becoming a certified EEG technologist.

**American Society of Electroencephalographic Technicians (ASET)—The Neurodiagnostic Society**

www.aset.org

ASET—The Neurodiagnostic Society is a professional association for people involved in the study and recording of electrical activity in the brain and nervous system. Its website provides news related to neurodiagnostic technologists, such as EEG technologists. It also provides information on schools that offer EEG technologist programs and scholarships that students can apply for.

## Hospital Careers

https://hospitalcareers.com

Hospital Careers is a website that allows people to search for health care jobs. Additionally, it provides information about various health care careers, including EEG technologist. The website provides information on what to focus on in high school to prepare for an EEG technologist path and what is involved in certification programs.

# Medical Robotics Engineer

## What Does a Medical Robotics Engineer Do?

Robots are becoming an integral part of the health care industry. In the 1980s the first robots in the medical field provided surgical assistance via robotic arm technologies. Today robotic systems combined with artificial intelligence (AI) and computer vision can assist with different types of surgeries. For example, surgeon-guided robots can perform hysterectomies (removal of the uterus) and bariatric surgeries (weight-loss surgery that decreases the size of the stomach). Robotic devices can also be programmed to perform orthopedic surgeries, such as knee and hip replacements. The possibilities are growing as the technology develops—and the professionals who are at the center of that development are medical robotics engineers.

A medical robotics engineer designs, builds, and tests the robotic systems that perform medical tasks. While many build robots that perform surgeries, others develop robots for different medical uses. Deanna Hood is a robotics engineer in Australia. She helped develop a

## A Few Facts

**Number of Jobs**
About 277,560 in 2021*

**Pay**
Median annual salary of $101,517 in 2023

**Educational Requirements**
Bachelor's degree in mechanical engineering, biomedical engineering, or similar field

**Personal Qualities**
Imaginative, mathematical, collaborative

**Work Settings**
Laboratories or offices

**Future Job Outlook**
Growth rate of 2 percent through 2031*

* This number is for mechanical engineers, which includes robotics engineers.

robot that prints skin for patients with severe burns. Human skin can usually make new cells to replace damage from minor burns. This does not happen with severe burns. Instead, healthy skin is grafted over damaged tissue to help with healing. Printed skin provides a source of skin for this purpose. "It was both rewarding and fascinating to work alongside surgeons to design a product to save patients' lives," Hood says. "Especially because I got to do it using robots, coding and other technology that I love."[11]

Other engineers are working on robotic devices used in telesurgeries. Telesurgery involves a surgeon in one location who is performing surgery on a patient in another location. This is made possible by advances in robotics, imaging, video, and sensors. In telesurgery, a robot performs the exact movements that surgeons make on controllers, via a high-speed internet connection. Xuanhe Zhao, a professor of mechanical engineering and civil and environmental engineering at the Massachusetts Institute of Technology, is among those working on robotic devices for telesurgeries. "We imagine, instead of transporting a patient from a rural area to a large city, they could go to a local hospital where nurses could set up this system," explains Zhao. "A neurosurgeon at a major medical center could watch live imaging of the patient and use the robot to operate [on the patient]. That's our future dream."[12]  Many other exciting possibilities are on the horizon.

## A Typical Workday

Tracy Accardi, vice president of research and development for surgical robotics at Medtronic, among the world's largest medical technology and services companies, leads teams of scientists and engineers involved in research and development of surgical robotics. She and her team are working on a robotics-assisted surgery system called the Hugo™. The Hugo is a modular system, meaning it can be moved from one operating room to another. It has four arms to use in surgeries. At the console, surgeons control the robotic arms with grip controllers and view what the Hugo's camera "sees" in the patient.

## A Student's Perspective

"I'm one of the first students taking the [medical robotics and artificial intelligence graduate-level] course. It's been really exciting and it's been a very interesting course. It's been quite varied. . . . Part of it is aspects of robotics and surgical robotics and another part is AI, machine learning, deep learning and how they can be implemented into the medical field. And you also can . . . look into computer vision, so there's a whole big range of different aspects of the course."

—Athena, postgraduate student in medical robotics and artificial intelligence at University College London

Quoted in UCL Physics and Biomedical Engineering, *What Is It like Studying on MSc Medical Robotics and Artificial Intelligence?*, YouTube, November 11, 2022. www .youtube.com/watch?v=AKRmdmEaPiY.

Accardi spends her days reviewing the data and results from various projects in the laboratories, meeting with the scientists and engineers for updates on the projects, and meeting with customers to ensure design requirements are established and met. Accomplishing this means understanding what their customers, who are physicians and hospital executives, need from the robots during surgeries. "[The design process] starts with interviewing hundreds and hundreds of physicians and hospital executives to understand what their challenges are,"[13] Accardi explains.

Information obtained from conversations with customers informs the design process. As an example, Accardi and her team have found that surgeons want flexibility with robotic systems. They want the ability to change components for one type of surgery to components that can be used in a different type of surgery. As a result of these conversations, Accardi's team developed four robotic arms. The surgical instruments the robotic arms use can be changed to work in different procedures, ranging from repairing a hole in a heart to a gastrectomy, in which a part of the stomach is removed. Ultimately, Accardi's day-to-day job focuses on collaborating with the customers and her scientists and engineers to develop quality products that best meet surgical needs.

## Education and Training

A high school student interested in pursuing this field should take higher-level mathematics and science courses, with specific courses in biology, anatomy, and calculus to prepare for college. Programming skills are also desirable since this career requires understanding and using coding to develop robotic computer systems. Working on robotics during free time or joining a robotics club at school will also help develop needed skills.

A career in this field requires at least a bachelor's degree in biomedical engineering, robotics, mechanical engineering, or a related field. Most professionals also have a master's or doctoral degree. During college, finding internships in the field can help one gain experience for the job search after graduation.

## Skills and Personality

Major skills required of medical robotics engineers include understanding mathematics, mechanics, and biology. Mathematics and mechanics are necessary to design and create robotic movements. Knowledge of biology is necessary for robotic systems that are used in health care. Engineers must understand human anatomy and physiology to develop systems that can perform surgeries.

Communication and collaboration are essential for this career field. Medical robotics engineers spend a lot of time talking to customers such as surgeons to understand their needs. These engineers also work closely with scientists and other engineers. Designing and developing robots for medical purposes is a team effort that includes electrical engineers, computer software experts, mechanical engineers, and doctors, among others.

The design and development process often involves trial and error. Imagination, resourcefulness, and problem-solving skills

Medical robotics engineers design, build, and test robotic systems that perform a variety of tasks. As part of the job, they review data and results from various projects and often confer with colleagues and clients.

help achieve successful outcomes. As an example, for years, when surgeons used a robotic system, they had to look down through a closed console at a screen as they controlled the robotic arms. Many consequently developed neck pain and headaches. With this information, engineers worked to develop a system with an open console. This allows surgeons to sit and look straight ahead at the console, providing a solution to the problem.

## Working Conditions

Many medical robotics engineers work in laboratories at companies or universities, specifically designing and creating robotic devices. They may wear safety equipment such as gloves and goggles when actually working on the development and use of their devices. During other times, when designing and planning, they use computers to create schematics, plans, and documentation of the design and testing.

Medical robotics engineers often work in a hybrid environment: working both independently and with teams. As an example, an

## Research on the Cusp

"Stroke is the number five cause of death and a leading cause of disability in the United States. If acute stroke can be treated within the first 90 minutes or so, survival rates increase significantly. If our [robotic worm that can navigate through brain blood vessels] can reverse blood vessel blockage within this 'golden hour' of opportunity, we can potentially avoid permanent brain damage—that is our hope."

—Xuanhe Zhao, associate professor of mechanical, civil, and environmental engineering at the Massachusetts Institute of Technology

Quoted in Mark Crawford, "Robotic Worm to Navigate Through Human Brain," American Society of Mechanical Engineers, October 28, 2019. www.asme.org.

engineer may be tasked with working on specific coding for the computer vision of a surgical robot and spend much time on his or her area of code. Then, he or she also needs to work with others who are coding different aspects of the computer vision to ensure the programs work together. Also, the computer vision team would need to work with the engineers developing the arms and their movements. All aspects of the robot need to work together, requiring collaboration of the engineers involved.

Engineers at companies that produce products generally work regular hours each week. However, because it is a competitive industry, the need to meet deadlines can be intense. As these deadlines approach, the result is often long work hours during the week and on weekends.

## Employers and Earnings

According to Glassdoor, in May 2023 the estimated total pay for a robotics engineer was $101,517 per year in the United States. Companies such as Johnson & Johnson, Medtronic, and Intuitive Surgical hire medical robotics engineers. All of these companies are working toward using the latest technology, specifically AI and computer vision, to advance the robotic systems used in surgeries. As an example, Johnson & Johnson recently received US Food and Drug Administration clearance for its VELYS, an orthopedic surgery robot that is table mounted and able to integrate into any operating room. This is used with hip replacement and knee replacement surgeries and known for its accurate cuts and control. Companies like Johnson & Johnson need medical robotics engineers to continue making advancements like this.

## Future Outlook

Robot-assisted procedures rose to 15.1 percent of all general surgeries in 2018, from 1.8 percent in 2012, according to a study published in a 2020 issue of the *Journal of the American Medical Association*. That number is increasing each year as hospitals invest more in these innovations and surgeons become more interested in their use. In its survey of surgeons, the consulting firm Bain & Company found that 78 percent are interested in surgical robotics, compared to only 53 percent who currently use them. This leaves open much room for the field to grow to satisfy the needs of hospitals and surgeons.

## Find Out More

**American Society of Mechanical Engineers (ASME)**

www.asme.org

This organization of eighty-five thousand members is dedicated to advancing engineering for society. Its website provides news and articles pertaining to engineering, including medical robotics engineering. A link to its magazine is also included. The "Students and Faculty" section includes information about school programs it sponsors and scholarships for college students.

**Coursera**

www.coursera.org

Coursera is a website that provides job information and learning online. The section on robotics engineering provides an overview of what robotics engineers do and how to work toward this career. It includes information on skills required and education needed to become a robotics engineer.

**IEEE Robotics & Automation Society**
www.ieee ras.org
This nonprofit organization was created to encourage the sharing of robotics and automation knowledge with members and society as a whole. Its website provides the latest news and advancements in robotics and automation, conferences, and member news. Additionally, it includes precollege recommendations for preparation to pursue a robotics career.

# Nuclear Medicine Technologist

## What Does a Nuclear Medicine Technologist Do?

The key to treating gallbladder disease, kidney blockages, cancer, and other illnesses and conditions is first to discover what the specific issue is. Nuclear medicine technologists play a key role in this process. Nuclear medicine involves the use of radioactive drugs given to patients in small doses to produce images of internal organs and bodily functions. Doctors use these images for diagnosis and treatment.

Nuclear medicine technologists administer the radioactive drugs, also called radiopharmaceuticals, or tracers, and use high-tech machines to create the images that doctors need to see. These technologists may also administer doses of radioactive drugs to patients for some forms of cancer treatment.

Nuclear medicine technologists explain the process to their patients to ensure they understand what will happen during the procedure and its purpose. Then they administer the tracers to the patients orally or by injection. The tracers travel through the patient's bloodstream to the specific organs or tissues that need imaging. The nuclear technologist then

## A Few Facts

**Number of Jobs**
About 18,900 in 2021

**Pay**
Median annual salary of about $78,700 in 2021

**Educational Requirements**
Associate's degree and certification or license

**Personal Qualities**
Empathetic, critical thinker, analytic

**Work Settings**
Hospitals, physician offices

**Future Job Outlook**
Growth rate of 2 percent through 2031

runs the scan. The scans are provided to radiologists, who then evaluate the results in an effort to determine the problem.

Mathew Silva is a nuclear medicine technologist in a New Mexico hospital. He became interested in pursuing a medical career after breaking bones more than once as a high school wrestler. Silva specifically was interested in the imaging part of patient care. "What we do is, we inject patients with radiopharmaceuticals to look at functionality of the body and we take a look and see what's happening,"[14] Silva says of his work.

Nuclear medicine technologists work with a variety of scanning devices. One is a positron-emission tomography (PET) scanner, which measures metabolic activity in the cells. PET scans are often used to diagnose or monitor cancer since cancer cells show a higher metabolic rate of activity compared to regular cells. Another scanning device operated by nuclear medicine technologists is a single-photon-emission computerized tomography scan. It creates 3-D images and is used to check functions such as blood flow to the heart, which can help determine whether there is cardiovascular disease.

As part of their job, nuclear medicine technologists sometimes administer radiopharmaceuticals prescribed by doctors as a treatment for cancer. Ericka Padilla-Morales works as a nuclear medicine technologist at the University of California, San Francisco, cancer center. Her job includes administering radioactive drugs to cancer patients. "We might be giving them a course of treatment similar to chemotherapy, but instead of using chemicals, we're using nuclear medicine,"[15] Padilla-Morales explains. Radiopharmaceuticals recognize tumor cells and, after injected intravenously, move to the tumor cells and cause the cells to shrink or die. Whether their work contributes to diagnosis or treatment, nuclear medicine technologists play an integral role in a patient's fight against illness.

## A Typical Workday

Stana Kuzmanovic works as a nuclear medicine technologist in an Alberta, Canada, health care clinic. At the clinic her role is to provide scans of patients so doctors can diagnose their health issues. She begins every day with preparation of equipment and materials. Kuzmanovic explains, "A typical day as a nuclear medical technologist starts with quality control. So, quality control is making sure that all the instruments that we use to measure, monitor, and image radiation . . . are working properly and then, once we're done, we need to begin [preparing] our tracers so we can inject and perform the studies [imagining scans] throughout that day."[16] To prepare the tracers for patients, Kuzmanovic checks that the radiopharmaceutical, which is in a vial, is intact and has not passed its expiration date. She adds a nonradioactive solution to the substance. Then she uses laboratory tests to ensure that the radiopharmaceutical solution is pure (with no contaminants) and safe to inject in the patient. Next she puts the specific doses, based on patients' sizes and other factors, into syringes and labels them.

Then Kuzmanovic begins seeing patients. She brings them into the room, explains the process to them, answers their questions, and makes sure they are comfortable. "One of the most challenging [parts of the day is] patients that come in in physical and emotional distress and you are trying to make them as comfortable as they can be, and try to make their experience as good as it can be,"[17] Kuzmanovic says. Once patients are settled, she injects them with tracers or provides them tracer drugs to swallow, has them lie down for the test, and runs the scanning equipment.

After a test is finished and the patient has left, Kuzmanovic cleans the machinery for the next patient. In between patients, she processes the data from the test, reviews the images, enhances them, and then gives them to the doctor, who will study the images and data to make a diagnosis. At the end of each workday, she checks herself, her workspace, and even the trash to make sure radiation levels do not exceed safety limits. For Kuzmanovic, a successful day is one in which she has been able to make the process go smoothly for patients and help them get through a stressful time in their lives.

## Education and Training

According to the Nuclear Medicine Technology Certification Board, as of 2020 at least thirty states require licensing, and each state has its specific requirements for obtaining a license. The requirements typically include obtaining at least an associate's degree or certificate in nuclear medicine technology and passing a certification test. Colleges and health care facilities throughout the nation offer nuclear medicine technology programs that result in an associate's degree or certificate in nuclear medicine technology. Additionally, these programs help students prepare for certification tests. The programs are a mix of classwork and practical experience in clinical settings. According to O*NET, a data organization sponsored by the US Department of Labor, in 2021, 63 percent of these technologists had associate's degrees and 22 percent had a bachelor's degree. After completing a degree, one can take the American Registry of Radiologic Technologists or the Nuclear Medicine Technology Certification Board certification exam. Passing either test results in certification.

While in high school, aspiring technologists should consider classes like calculus, chemistry, biology, physics, computer

## Different Functions

"We do a bunch of different really cool stuff . . . so we also do whole body bone scans for patients with cancer to see if their cancer has metastasized. We do triple phase bone scans to see if someone's knee or hip replacements are loosened or infected. We do gallbladder studies to show if someone has acute or chronic cholecystitis . . . so we get to do a lot of . . . cool studies to show the radiologist how everything is functioning within the body."

—Amber McGee, nuclear medicine technologist

Amber McGee, *Nuclear Medicine Technologist*, YouTube, 2022. www.youtube.com /watch?v=LaMgUIiWIoY.

programming, and anatomy. These classes will help prepare students for courses such as computer processing and image enhancement, radiation safety, nuclear medicine, and anatomy, which are typically part of nuclear medicine technologist programs.

## Skills and Personality

Nuclear medicine technologists work directly with patients. It is not uncommon for those patients to be worried or scared about the procedure, their overall health, or both. Interaction with patients requires someone who is calm, personable, professional, and compassionate. The nuclear medicine technologist might not be able to ease a patient's fears about his or her overall health, but the technologist can make sure that the imaging process goes smoothly and professionally.

Those entering this field should be interested in and capable of learning the different sciences needed to understand the field. Padilla-Morales was a teacher, but after watching her aunt go through cancer treatment and undergo nuclear imaging scans, she realized it was time to change careers. She decided to become a nuclear medicine technologist because it included her two main interests. "When I [learned about] nuclear medicine I saw that it combined my love of science with my love of people as an educator," Padilla-Morales recalls. "And I thought . . . I get to combine these two great things that I . . . enjoy."[18]

Because the field is using the latest in nuclear medicine for diagnosis and treatment, it is important that nuclear medicine technologists stay current in their field. This means they should continue to actively read and learn about the latest advancements. "I think one of the greatest challenges about my career is that it's constantly evolving so we're asked to constantly keep learning,"[19] says Padilla-Morales.

## Working Conditions

According to the Bureau of Labor Statistics (BLS), 68 percent of nuclear medicine technologists work in hospitals, providing scans to help doctors diagnose patients. Their hours may include nights or twelve-hour shifts, depending on the hospital's schedule. There also may be days when they are on call and come in as needed.

Because they work with radioactive materials, they wear gloves and other shielding devices as needed. As a precaution, they also wear badges that measure radiation levels. Their radiation exposure is recorded to ensure levels do not exceed what is safe. The job also requires stamina and good physical strength because there is much standing and walking. Often, they may need to help patients sit, stand, or get on and off beds and may need to push a wheelchair or gurney.

## Employers and Earnings

The majority of nuclear medicine technologists work in hospitals, but some also work in outpatient clinics, private practices, and other medical facilities. Those who get additional training or education often command higher pay. They might advance to lead technologist, research technologist, manager, or educator. Certain states pay higher salaries on average than the national mean of approximately $79,000, according to the BLS. For example, as of 2021 the average annual salary for nuclear medicine technologists in California was $106,810. Additionally, the setting where one works impacts pay, since those who work in outpatient care centers receive $125,920 on average compared to about $78,700 in hospitals.

## Future Outlook

The BLS predicts that this career field will continue to grow at an average pace of about 2 percent. As the American population ages, the demand for testing and other health-related procedures will also increase. This will lead to a need for more health technologists of all types and open the way for young people who want to actively use technology while still engaging with people.

## Find Out More

**American Registry of Radiologic Technologists (ARRT)**
www.arrt.org
The AART is a credentialing organization that provides certification in different radiologic disciplines, including for nuclear medicine technologists. Its website provides information about certification exams, news related to the profession, and a search tool for educational programs. There is also a section on scholarships and grants.

**Nuclear Medicine Technology Certification Board (NMTCB)**
https://nmtcb.org
The NMTCB is an organization that provides licenses to nuclear medicine technologists. Its website provides relevant information on certification requirements, surveys of salaries in the field, what technologists are tasked with doing, and a newsletter with the latest information on the field.

**U.S. News & World Report**

https://money.usnews.com/careers/best-jobs/nuclear-medicine
-technologist

In its career listings, *U.S. News & World Report* includes information about nuclear medicine technologist jobs. The website provides salary expectations, job openings, reviews of the job, and news related to the career.

# Medical Laboratory Scientist

## What Does a Medical Laboratory Scientist Do?

On any given day, doctors order tests on blood, urine, and tissue samples for routine health checks and to aid diagnosis of any number of illnesses. All of these biological specimens undergo analysis in a laboratory. That analysis is done by medical laboratory scientists. According to the Centers for Disease Control and Prevention, an estimated 60 to 70 percent of all decisions regarding a patient's diagnosis and subsequent treatment are determined on the basis of the results of tests and analyses performed by medical laboratory scientists.

Testing and analysis of tissue samples, bodily fluids, and cells is done with equipment such as microscopes, hematology analyzers, and incubators. Studying specimens under the microscope can reveal the presence of fungus or bacteria. Hematology analyzers are machines that can be used to test blood for red blood cell count and white blood cell count. Incubators allow medical laboratory scientists to grow cells that can then be studied to determine whether certain bacteria are present. Medical laboratory scientists analyze the test results, record

## A Few Facts

**Number of Jobs**
About 329,200 in 2021

**Pay**
Median annual salary of $57,800 in 2021

**Educational Requirements**
Bachelor's degree, preferably in a science

**Personal Qualities**
Precise, focused, inquisitive

**Work Settings**
Hospital or medical facilities, diagnostic laboratories

**Future Job Outlook**
Growth rate of 7 percent through 2031

the results in patient records, and provide the results to doctors. Their results can be a crucial part of determining the cause of a patient's health problems and help doctors diagnose and treat the disease or injury.

Responsibility for calibrating and maintaining the microscopes, incubators, and other equipment also falls to these scientists. They do standard maintenance, such as sterilizing equipment after each use and regularly calibrating the equipment to ensure accurate results. They also troubleshoot when problems arise. For example, if an incubator is not achieving the correct temperature, they check to see whether there is a part failure or a seal is broken.

Unlike many people working in the health care industry, medical laboratory scientists do not work directly with patients. For this reason, those who are interested in a medical field but not drawn to patient care may find this a good fit. Amanda Michel is a certified medical laboratory scientist who works for a nonprofit health care company in the Midwest. She tests patient samples for different medical conditions. "[I wanted something in] the medical career [field], but I . . . didn't want to do direct patient care. So, I was going through different [college catalogs] and I found a degree in medical technology," Michel recalls. "It's all working in the laboratory using science, and still being able to be in a hospital or clinical setting where you're helping patients, but not directly."[20]

## A Typical Workday

Dominique Larae is a medical laboratory scientist who works for a hospital in Atlanta, Georgia. She works in the hospital's pathology department, where she tests specimens such as blood and urine samples taken from hospital patients. The results of those tests can give doctors important clues to ailments affecting the liver, kidneys, heart, urinary tract, and more. She feels like her job is that of an investigator who is looking to see whether there is anything out of the ordinary in the laboratory tests. Sometimes she may be testing for a specific ailment, such as hepatitis. Other

## A Drop of Blood

"You'll get a hematology slide where you're looking at the inside of somebody's body. You're looking at their blood and you can see all of these different things that's going on with them. You could see lots of white blood cells, meaning they have an infection. You could see that their red blood cells are too small or too big or they're not the right size and . . . I just think it's so neat that you can then see what's going on with them by just a drop of their blood."

—Amanda Michel, medical laboratory scientist

Quoted in Medical Laboratory Science Careers, *Medical Laboratory Scientist Interview—Is the Career for You?*, YouTube, 2021. www.youtube.com/watch ?v=Rn32ubVxK6M.

times she may be looking at blood results to help determine what could potentially be the cause of a person feeling excessively tired or dizzy.

Larae explains that most of her day is spent in the laboratory working on the samples provided by patients. "One thing about this job is that I get to help patients behind the scenes so I can provide my lab findings to help patients get what they need without ever having to see them," Larae says. "I do work closely with the phlebotomists and nurses who are trained to collect the blood and other body fluids I need in order to do testing."[21] Her interactions with the phlebotomists and nurses include instructing them on how to collect and label the specimens.

The lab work Larae performs is often a search to see whether a patient is afflicted with a disease or ailment. In her tests she may be looking to see how a sample reacts with a specific chemical, the number of red cells present in a specimen, or a cell's shape to determine what is happening to the patient. "For example . . . I could see sickle cell anemia by looking at the shape of the red blood cells and I can identify crystals and body fluids that are

Medical laboratory scientists test and analyze biological specimens including tissue samples, bodily fluids, and cells. The results of these tests assist doctors in diagnosing and treating all sorts of health conditions.

present in certain diseases. . . . That's just a few things that we can investigate with just the microscope,"[22] Larae explains. The majority of her day is spent conducting tests, but she also spends part of it recording the results and providing them to the doctors. Her goal is to accurately analyze results in a timely manner so patients can receive answers and care.

## Education and Training

High school students who are interested in this career should take science courses with laboratory work, such as biology and chemistry. This will help them determine whether laboratory work is interesting to them. Volunteering at a local hospital is also a way to gain experience in a medical setting, which can help students decide whether it is to their liking and provide them experience to help them get into a related program.

Medical laboratory scientists typically obtain a bachelor's degree in clinical or medical laboratory science, biomedical science, biology, or biochemistry from an academic institution that is accredited by the National Accrediting Agency for Clinical Laboratory Sciences. Many states require medical laboratory scientists to be certified. Most certification boards require a bachelor's degree, experience in a laboratory and/or completion of a medical laboratory science program, and passing an exam. The exam covers subjects such as blood group systems, microbiology, chemistry, and bodily fluid analysis. Even if a state does not require certification to work as a medical laboratory scientist, most employers prefer applicants that are certified. Certifications should come from a recognized professional association, such as the American Medical Technologists or American Society for Clinical Pathology.

## Skills and Personality

People's lives depend on the accuracy of medical tests, so being a precise and careful person is a must for this job. Much of the work of medical laboratory scientists consists of conducting tests, analyzing test results, and determining the results based on what the tests show. Because of this, medical laboratory scientists must be analytical as they consider all of the facts from the samples and use their knowledge to determine the results.

An inquisitive nature is also beneficial for medical laboratory scientists as they evaluate various lab test results aimed at finding the cause of a patient's symptoms. This will also help them continue learning in their field and keep up with the latest advances. These scientists should also be interested in and have an aptitude for the life sciences, which is the study of microorganisms, plants, and animals and their bodily functions and development.

## Working Conditions

Most of the workday for medical laboratory scientists takes place in a laboratory. Because they work with blood, other bodily fluids, and human tissue, they wear protective masks, gloves, and goggles. This helps them avoid direct exposure that could lead to infection.

As with many health care jobs, this one can be demanding. Patients might be in the emergency room (ER), intensive care unit (ICU), neonatal intensive care unit (NICU), or elsewhere in the hospital awaiting results of their tests. Whatever their conditions, medical laboratory scientists understand that the work they do can affect another person's health and life—in good ways and bad. Larae explains:

> It can be pretty stressful . . . at a given time during a shift I am responsible for testing and reporting results on patients all over the hospital from the ER to the ICU or labor/delivery, NICU . . . cardiology, pediatrics . . . whatever other department you can think of. It's our responsibility in the lab to make sure each and every patient gets results in a timely manner. It's also on us to make sure that patients are getting accurate tests.[23]

## Employers and Earnings

The Bureau of Labor Statistics (BLS) reports that 44 percent of these scientists work in hospitals, while 22 percent are located at medical and diagnostic laboratories. The remainder work in university laboratories, outpatient clinics, and private doctor's offices. Their average salary is $57,800, but this can vary according to experience, location, and credentials. According to the American Society for Clinical Pathology's 2021 Wage Survey of Medical Laboratories in the United States, large hospitals associated with universities pay the highest salaries for medical laboratory scientists. Moving forward, a medical laboratory scientist can work toward higher-level jobs such as being a lead medical laboratory scientist or director of a laboratory.

## Future Outlook

Medical laboratory scientist jobs are growing at a rate higher than the average. As the American population ages, the demand for

## Night Shift

"I like the [night] shift. I work independently on my own or with one other person. . . . I'm pretty much responsible for everything going on [at the laboratory] . . . I'm able to work independently and figure problems out on my own."

—Rosa Perez, medical laboratory scientist

Rosa Perez, *Day in the Life of a Medical Laboratory Scientist*, YouTube, 2021. www.youtube.com/watch?v=RSZnl_WKyCE.

all sorts of laboratory tests will also increase. The BLS estimates that through 2031 this career will grow at the rate of 7 percent. With new techniques and technology in medical laboratory testing constantly developing, this field is one for a person who wants to work hands-on with the latest equipment and computer analysis programs in a medical setting. "The microbiology lab particularly is in a renaissance right now," explains Amanda Reed, Medical Laboratory Science program director at Saint Louis University. "The techniques and testing methods that are being employed in the microbiology lab have changed so much since I stepped foot in the lab in 2012. It's like night and day and so you know it's challenging and it's rewarding. You know that you're helping people."[24]

## Find Out More
### American Medical Technologists
https://americanmedtech.org
This organization provides certification processes for those in laboratory fields, including medical laboratory scientists. Its website provides a career development how-to for medical laboratory scientists and the route to become certified through its association. It has a job search tool, ways to network with peers for those in the field, and news in the field.

## National Accrediting Agency for Clinical Laboratory Sciences (NAACLS)

www.naacls.org

The NAACLS is an accrediting organization for people in clinical laboratory sciences fields. Its website provides information on its accreditation process, including for medical laboratory scientists. There is a student section that provides links to information on scholarships available for those pursuing laboratory sciences and a search tool for laboratory science programs nationwide.

## WebMD

www.webmd.com/a-to-z-guides/what-is-medical-laboratory-scientist

WebMD is an online resource providing health information from experts. Its section called "What Is a Medical Laboratory Scientist?" explains the job tasks, education requirements, and how these scientists impact patient care.

# Sonographer

## What Does a Sonographer Do?

An ultrasound, also called a sonogram, is an imaging test that shows the structures inside the body. The sonogram equipment transmits high-intensity sound waves into the body to produce the needed images. An ultrasound can reveal the health of a fetus during pregnancy, show whether a lump is a cyst or tumor, and find blockages in blood vessels. Because an ultrasound is noninvasive and does not use radiation, doctors often use this as their first tool in finding the source of a health problem or assessing a potential health issue. The high-frequency sound waves of ultrasounds are safe, so it is a test that can be used on all patients—from pregnant women to babies, children, and seniors—with little risk. Sonographers conduct the tests using the ultrasound equipment.

An ultrasound is done with the help of a handheld device known as a transducer. Sonographers roll the transducer along the skin of the belly, breast, or other part of the patient's body. The sonographer first applies a thin layer of gel to the skin, and the transducer transmits sound

## A Few Facts

**Number of Jobs**
About 140,400 in 2021*

**Pay**
Median annual salary of $77,740 in 2021

**Educational Requirements**
Associate's degree and certification

**Personal Qualities**
Meticulous, mechanically inclined, communicative

**Work Settings**
Hospitals, medical facilities

**Future Job Outlook**
Growth rate of 10 percent through 2031

* This number includes sonographers and cardiovascular technologists and technicians.

waves through the gel and into the body. The images develop as the sound waves bounce off internal organs and return to a computer. Sonographers watch the images and adjust as they are scanning to obtain the specific views ordered by the doctor. They are also trained to analyze the ultrasound images and provide their results and analysis to radiologists. The radiologists use these images to diagnose and treat many medical conditions.

Because there are so many ultrasound uses, many sonographers specialize in certain areas, like the female reproductive system, abdomen, or heart. No matter what area they specialize in, sonographers must be tech-savvy enough to apply this sophisticated technology to manipulate and optimize the images. However, they also must be personable enough to put patients who might be nervous or uncomfortable at ease.

## A Typical Workday

As a cardiovascular sonographer at Nebraska Medicine, Samantha spends much of her work time conducting ultrasounds of hearts and arteries for cardiologists and vascular surgeons. "I like the fast pace of the med center, working as a team,"[25] she says.

Some of the patients Samantha works with come to the hospital clinic as outpatients, so they get the ultrasound and then leave. Others stay in the hospital, which means she brings a portable ultrasound machine to the patient's room and does the imaging there. Sometimes she encounters challenges. For example, with an obese patient it can be difficult to find a position that allows for detailed images of the heart. In instances like this, the sonographer must try to move the transducer to different locations to get a better image.

Tessa Kay is also a sonographer, but she works in a private medical practice. When she arrives at work, her first task is to refill the bottles that hold the gel used to help produce clearer images. Then she wipes down the ultrasound machine, the bed, and other spaces to ensure everything is sterile. Following that, she puts fresh sheets and a pillow on the bed. After reviewing her list of patients and scans required for the day, she reviews her first patient's chart, including his or symptoms and medical history. If the patient has been to the office before for an ultrasound involving an abnormality such as a cyst or tumor, she will look at the earlier scans. This helps her identify the exact location for the new scan, which will allow the doctor to see whether changes have occurred.

Most sonographers perform nine to ten sonograms a day, and each one takes approximately twenty to forty-five minutes. During this time sonographers usually do not aim for one perfect image. Instead, they try to get multiple images taken from various angles to give the doctor many views. "You'll be a better tech because you're not worried about one image," Kay says. "You're not taking five minutes to take one image of the liver. You're not overthinking that one image. It's best to take the image the best you can and take multiple images and angles of whatever organ you're looking at in order to help the radiologists see what you're seeing."[26]

Kay also interacts with the radiologists reviewing her scans. There are times when a radiologist wants her opinions and insight regarding what she saw. This helps the radiologist make a diagnosis and ultimately helps the patient. Her advice is to stay calm and be honest when talking with a radiologist, which may be intimidating to newer sonographers. She says to remember that you are the radiologist's "eyes" since you took the images, and what you say will help him or her help the patient.

## Education and Training

Many employers require candidates to have completed a professional sonography certification, which can be obtained through various programs. Most sonography programs lead to an associate's degree and preparation for a certification exam. Community colleges often have two-year associate's degree programs in sonography. This is the most common path for people seeking to become sonographers. Sonography programs include classes in anatomy, physiology, ultrasound imaging, and actual hands-on clinical training in using the equipment and interpreting sonographic images.

For high school students, taking science courses such as anatomy, biology, and chemistry will help prepare them for the courses needed to become a sonographer. This is because the courses in any sonography program are predominately sciences, with a focus on anatomy.

## Skills and Personality

Technical skills, attention to detail, and writing skills are important attributes for a sonographer. Sonographers need to have technical ability since they are responsible for using, maintaining, and troubleshooting ultrasound equipment. They must ensure their images are detailed, of exactly the area required, and of good quality. Sonographers must be meticulous in their write-ups and analyses because these are relied on by doctors.

Because sonographers interact directly with patients, good communication and empathy are important, along with being in good physical shape. They need to be able to explain the process

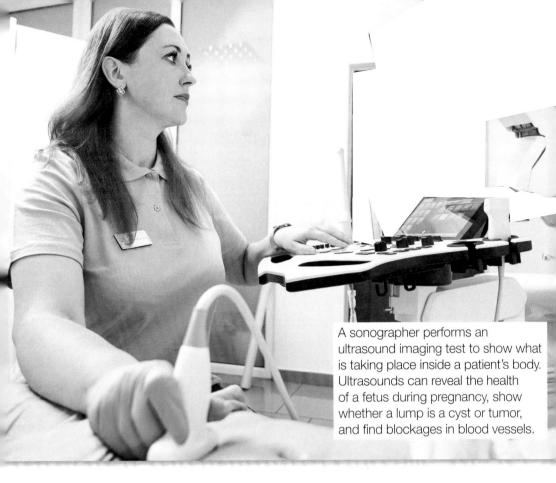

A sonographer performs an ultrasound imaging test to show what is taking place inside a patient's body. Ultrasounds can reveal the health of a fetus during pregnancy, show whether a lump is a cyst or tumor, and find blockages in blood vessels.

to patients, answer any questions, and ease any fears patients may have about the procedure. Sonographers also help patients by moving them into the correct position and helping them on and off the bed. Amanda's years as a sonographer at Cleveland Clinic have led her to the conclusion that when you work with patients all day long, being in good physical shape and having empathy is essential. "To succeed in ultrasound, you will need to be . . . [physically] healthy and have no severe injuries preventing you from standing for long periods of time and the moving of patients," Amanda says. "Having a good bedside manner is also an excellent skill to have in any healthcare profession."[27]

## Working Conditions

About 60 percent of sonographers work in hospitals. Hospital work usually involves at least some days of being on call. While

## Not Just Pictures

"There are a million and one things that can go wrong in utero and it is me, and only me, that has that tremendous burden placed on my shoulders as I scan intently as to not miss anything. The images we take and what we report are what the doctor sees, so if we miss a finding on an exam, guess what? The doctor will not have seen it and you and your baby can have a condition that will go undiagnosed."

—Sarah, a sonographer specializing in fetal ultrasounds

Quoted in Baby Gizmo, "Ultrasounds: What Your Sonographer Actually Does," 2019. https://babygizmo.com.

on call, a sonographer must be ready to return to the hospital at any time of the day or night, even on weekends or holidays, if an emergency ultrasound is needed. Regular shifts also may be during the day, at night, and from four to twelve hours each, depending on the hospital. Other sonographers work in doctor offices, diagnostic facilities, and outpatient centers, and their hours are more predictable, with Monday to Friday workdays. In all settings, there may be part-time options available.

While sonographers do not deal with radiation, they are exposed to potential biohazards such as bodily secretions from some patients. For this reason, they wash their hands throughout the day and continuously sterilize equipment and the area where they work. Additionally, they move a lot throughout the day, helping patients get into position and using the ultrasound scanner to get the exact areas on the patient, so they can experience injuries from repetitive motions.

## Employers and Earnings

Most sonographers are employed by hospitals and medical facilities. The average pay, according to the Bureau of Labor Statistics (BLS), is $77,740 a year. Surgical hospitals typically pay more; the average pay at a surgical hospital is about $84,340 a year.

What area sonographers focus on also impacts their salaries. Neurosonography, specializing in brain images, is the highest-paid sonographer specialty. The average pay of a neurosonographer is $54 per hour or $112,320 per year. Breast and cardiac sonography are also highly paid, since these are areas where accurate images are important to diagnose potentially serious diseases. Also, sonographers have the potential to earn more if they choose to advance to higher positions in their field. In a hospital setting, sonographers have the possibility of taking on lead and management positions in the department. Additionally, they can go into education, teaching other sonographers or working with sonography manufacturers in sales and training.

## Future Outlook

Sonographers will continue to be in need, according to the BLS, since the field is expected to grow at a faster-than-average rate of 10 percent through 2031. As the American population ages, the demand for testing and other health-related procedures such as sonograms will increase. Amanda has seen the use of sonography grow during her career, both from technological advances and increased use in wellness care. "Over the last five years of being a sonographer, the demand has grown immensely," Amanda says of sonography. "Physicians are often ordering ultrasounds for routine care as well as emergent situations. The technology is enhancing the quality of our work, and we are able to scan more patients than ever. The machines are forever evolving, becoming more detailed to provide the best imaging possible."[28] With these advances and changes, future sonographers have the potential to enjoy a long and interesting career in health care.

# Find Out More

## American Society of Echocardiography (ASE)

www.asecho.org

The ASE is dedicated to advancing cardiovascular ultrasound and promoting education, research, and innovation in the field. Its website has links to journals about the field, how to become a member, news in the field, and student scholarship applications.

## Commission on Accreditation of Allied Health Education Programs (CAAHEP)

www.caahep.org

The CAAHEP provides accreditation to different programs for various medical fields. Its website provides a search for accredited programs, including advanced cardiovascular sonography and diagnostic medical sonography, as well as specializations. It also provides a student section with frequently asked questions about certifications and the importance of attending a certified program.

## Society of Diagnostic Medical Sonography

www.sdms.org

This organization was developed to promote, advance, and educate both members and the medical community about diagnostic medical sonography. Its website includes the latest technology updates and news in the career field. It also includes career surveys, salary surveys, and basic information about getting into the career field.

# Source Notes

## Introduction: Technology in Medicine Equals Jobs

1. Ashok K. Harnal, "Will Artificial Intelligence Take Over Health-care Jobs?," *Economic Times* (Mumbai, India), March 10, 2023. https://economictimes.indiatimes.com.
2. Madhukar Pai, "Engineers Are Unsung Heroes of Global Health," *Forbes*, May 5, 2022. www.forbes.com.
3. Quoted in Kenneth Parker, "MARCA: Interview with a Certified Nuclear Technologist on Medicare Disbursements," MTS, 2023. www.medicaltechnologyschools.com.

## Biomedical Engineer

4. Quoted in Johns Hopkins Biomedical Engineering, *Natalia Trayanova—Pioneering Cardiovascular Engineering*, YouTube, 2018. www.youtube.com/watch?v=bX62KNOfdBs&t=10s5.
5. Quoted in Crazy Medusa, *Day in the Life of a Biomedical Engineer—Layoffs & Is Biomedical a Safe Option?*, YouTube, 2023, www.youtube.com/watch?v=WUsqKzZ3Uvw&t=661s.
6. Alexa Perozo, *Day in the Life of a Biomedical Engineer*, YouTube, 2022. www.youtube.com/watch?v=0GyvH2l1ZVg.
7. Quoted in Navigate the Circuit, "Irene Bacalocostantis." https://navigate.aimbe.org.

## EEG Technologist

8. Cathy Konold, "EEG Tech: My Typical Day at Work," LinkedIn, March 18, 2020. www.linkedin.com.
9. Konold, "EEG Tech."
10. Quoted in Alberta Health Services, *AHS Careers EEG Technologist*, YouTube, 2019. www.youtube.com/watch?v=1pdZawxjvLl.

## Medical Robotics Engineer

11. Quoted in Jacob Biba, "What Does a Robotics Engineer Do?," Built In, April 12, 2023. https://builtin.com.
12. Quoted in Jennifer Chu, "Joystick-Operated Robot Could Help Surgeons Treat Stroke Remotely," *MIT News*, April 13, 2022. https://news.mit.edu.

13. Quoted in Alice Ferng, "Medical Robotics and the Future of Surgery: Interview with Tracy Accardi, VP of R&D for Medtronic Surgical Robotics," Medgadget, March 16, 2021. www.medgadget.com.

## Nuclear Medicine Technologist
14. Quoted in New Mexico PBS, *What It Takes—Matthew Silva, Nuclear Medicine Technologist*, YouTube, 2022. www.youtube.com/watch?v=8Euh3v90hi4.
15. Quoted in UCSF Cancer, *Career Paths: Nuclear Medicine Technologist*, YouTube, 2021. www.youtube.com/watch?v=vFW8LdeDgftY.
16. Quoted in Alis, *Occupational Video—Nuclear Medicine Technologist*, YouTube, 2019. www.youtube.com/watch?v=TCNvM0fTm4E.
17. Quoted in Alis, *Occupational Video—Nuclear Medicine Technologist*.
18. Quoted in UCSF Cancer, *Career Paths*.
19. Quoted in UCSF Cancer, *Career Paths*.

## Medical Laboratory Scientist
20. Quoted in Medical Laboratory Science Careers, *Medical Laboratory Scientist Interview—Is the Career for You?*, YouTube, 2021. www.youtube.com/watch?v=Rn32ubVxK6M.
21. Dominique Larae, *What Does a Medical Laboratory Scientist Do? Role, Patient Care & Misconceptions (FAQ)*, YouTube, 2023. www.youtube.com/watch?v=qb8WJA-_Vpk.
22. Larae, *What Does a Medical Laboratory Scientist Do?*
23. Larae, *What Does a Medical Laboratory Scientist Do?*
24. Quoted in Medical Laboratory Science Careers, *Medical Laboratory Scientist Career Decision*, YouTube, 2021. www.youtube.com/watch?v=E86P_XfelwM.

## Sonographer
25. Quoted in Nebraska Medicine Nebraska Medical Center, *My Job in a Minute: Cardiovascular Sonographer—Nebraska Medicine*, YouTube, 2023. www.youtube.com/watch?v=qpcp3j9l_LY.
26. Tessa Kay, *What I Learned as a Sonographer *a Year Later*—the Good, the Bad & What Other Techs Don't Tell You*, YouTube, 2021. www.youtube.com/watch?v=K4qOBEqd9YY.
27. Quoted in Cleveland Clinic, "Meet a Sonographer: Amanda," 2023. https://my.clevelandclinic.org.
28. Quoted in Cleveland Clinic, "Meet a Sonographer."

# Interview with a Sonographer

Meaghan Rissmann is a sonographer in Oklahoma City, Oklahoma. She works full time at a hospital that specializes in heart ailments and part time at an echocardiography lab that performs heart sonograms. She graduated with a bachelor's degree in medical imaging and radiological sciences from the University of Oklahoma in 2021. She answered questions about her job via email in July 2023.

**Q: Why did you become a sonographer?**

**A:** I wanted to become a sonographer because I had to have an echo[cardiogram] done when I was 15. I didn't even know that it was an ultrasound before I got there! I didn't know that ultrasounds could be done on anything other than babies. The sonographer that did my exam was so kind and explained everything to me and let me guess what anatomy we were looking at. Then, she had a sonography student come in the room and he had graduated from the same small town that I was going to school in! We all talked the whole way through the exam and when I went home to research sonography afterward, I fell in love. I just knew it was what I was meant to do.

**Q: Can you describe your typical workday?**

**A:** I work three 12-hour shifts per week in the hospital but there are so many options for sonographers! Some work five-day 8-hour shifts. Some work four-day 10-hour shifts. Some work in outpatient clinics and some even do mobile ultrasounds and drive around with their equipment all day! It's a very versatile field and there are so many different kinds of ultrasound. I mostly do echocardiograms of the heart but some sonographers only scan pregnant people, some only scan liver or kidney transplants. Some even scan nerves and muscles! There's definitely something for everyone that's interested!

**Q: What do you like most about your job?**
**A:** I love the field itself. Sonography is a really physics-heavy field so there's a ton of evolution happening all the time! The machines keep getting better and better and the field keeps expanding. Ultrasound became medically diagnostic around the 1970s and it's so cool to see how far we've come since then!

**Q: What do you like least about your job?**
**A:** I think that a lot of people underestimate sonographers. It's very user dependent, more so than the other imaging modalities, and it can take a decent amount of strength to get a good image! It's not uncommon for people to minimize our work as "just taking pictures." I've had a lot of people tell me that the field will become wiped out by advancing technology but I don't see that happening anytime soon. So sometimes you just have to have thick skin.

**Q: What was the most interesting project or task you worked on?**
**A:** We do a lot of work in the operating room and some of the most interesting things I've helped with are heart valve replacements! I help the doctors get images of the bad valve and take a bunch of measurements so that they know what size prosthetic to use. It's incredibly interesting to watch them work. Valve prosthetics have come a long way too and it's so exciting to see every time!

**Q: What personal qualities do you find valuable for this type of work?**
**A:** I think you definitely need to be patient to be a sonographer. Practice makes perfect and it can be tricky in the beginning. There are always new things to learn, as well! You definitely have to be

willing to take the time to sit down and learn new things whenever the opportunity presents itself. There's never a dull moment!

**Q: What advice do you have for students who might be interested in this as a career?**

**A:** I think that students that are interested in sonography should call some hospitals that specialize in different areas of sonography! Most hospitals will let students shadow their departments. Try out a general abdominal lab, a prenatal lab, and an echo lab to see what the best fit for you is! Another thing . . . do your research on the schools you apply to!! If the school you attend isn't accredited, it can be tricky to pass your board exams after graduation because there are a lot of extra steps you have to go through. This is becoming a more and more common problem for new sonographers.

# Other Jobs in Medical Technology

Anesthesia technician
Biological technician
Blood bank technologist
Cardiovascular technologist
Clinical laboratory scientist
Cytogenic technologist
DNA analyst
Hematology technologist
Histotechnologists
Laboratory assistant
Microbiologist
Microbiology technician
Medical equipment technician
Medical laboratory assistant
Medical laboratory technician

Medical scientist
Medical technologist
Molecular biology technologist
Neurologist
Neuroscientist
Nuclear medicine physicist
Nuclear pharmacist
Nuclear technician
Pathologist
Pathologist assistant
Phlebotomy technician
Radiation technologist
Radiation therapist
Robotics engineer
Surgical technologist

Editor's note: The online *Occupational Outlook Handbook* of the US Department of Labor's Bureau of Labor Statistics is an excellent source of information on jobs in hundreds of career fields, including many of those listed here. The *Occupational Outlook Handbook* may be accessed online at www.bls.gov/ooh.

# Index

*Note: Boldface page numbers indicate illustrations.*

# Picture Credits

# About the Author

Leanne K. Currie-McGhee has written educational books for over two decades and loves what she does. She lives in Norfolk, Virginia, with her husband, Keith, two children, Grace and Sol, and dog, Delilah.